LIFE
INTERRUPTED

FINDING PEACE IN THE DETOURS, DEAD ENDS, AND DISAPPOINTMENTS

CREATED BY TIERCE GREEN

GOOD FEED
MEDIA

LIFE INTERRUPTED

Published by **Good Feed Media**

Copyright 2025 Tierce Green Ministries, Inc.

All rights reserved.

ISBN: 979-8-9921538-3-5

This book supports the video content created and presented by Tierce Green. There are eight sessions in the series. Each session is about 25 minutes.

Video sessions for this series are completely FREE within the Good Feed Media App. There is no obligation to pay anything, but you have the opportunity to help us KEEP IT FREE by paying it forward.

Order additional copies of this resource and high-definition videos of this series for public viewing from Good Feed Media.

GOOD FEED
M E D I A
FREE APP. FREE CONTENT.

ORDER RESOURCES AND DOWNLOAD THE APP AT GOODFEEDMEDIA.COM

Good Feed Media is a division of Tierce Green Ministries, Inc.

Video production by Layne Laughter.

Interior photo by Katie Moum on Unsplash.

Distributed by:

Tierce Green Ministries, Inc.

The Woodlands, TX

tiercegreen.com

TABLE OF
CONTENTS

ABOUT THE CONTENT

When the circumstances of life are uncertain, we want to know for what cause, reason, or purpose. "Why?" is a question we never stop asking.

We can tell God exactly what we're feeling, not what we think He wants us to feel. We can ask Him anything. However, we need to understand the Power of Why. It can lead us to a deeper faith and expand our understanding of God's character and sovereignty, or it can sink us like an anchor around our neck. This tiny three-letter word is debilitating when it demands an explanation that we think will restore our control of the circumstances.

Everything happens for a reason. It's a commonly used saying to explain unexpected circumstances and manage fear and anxiety when life is interrupted. Those who use it don't necessarily believe in God, at least not the God of the Bible. It hints at a belief in something bigger than themselves—a reason they can't see when they're in the moment, but they hope it will appear.

Jesus promises His peace in the midst of trouble. His peace is in a class to itself. It's bulletproof. He tells us exactly where to find it. And that is where these eight sessions will take us. Along the way, we will discover that the best question is not, "WHERE is God in all this?" but "WHO is God in all this?"

Video sessions of this content can be freely accessed on the Good Feed Media App. Learn more and download at GOODFEEDMEDIA.COM

ABOUT THE AUTHOR

Tierce Green has over 45 years of professional ministry experience, including 30 years as a full-time speaker for conferences and retreats and 15 years of local church ministry. He served as a Student Pastor in a church of 1,200 and an Executive Pastor in a church of 12,000, where he led over a thousand men each week for seven years in a seasonal gathering called The Quest.

Tierce is on the presentation team of 33 The Series for Authentic Manhood, which has reached over three million men worldwide. He is the Director of Authentic Manhood Initiative, coaching leaders to reach men with the principles of biblical manhood. He is also the Director of **Good Feed Media**, creating quality disciple-making content freely available on the Good Feed Media App.

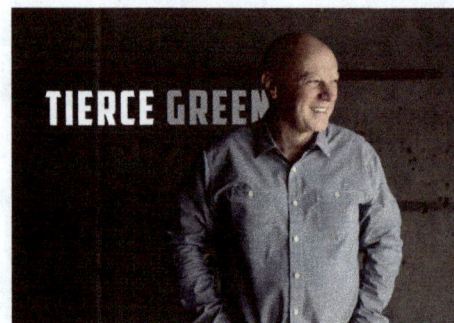

Tierce and his wife, Dana, have one daughter, Anna, and live in The Woodlands, TX.

1

THE POWER OF WHY

LIFE
INTERRUPTED

I. THE WHY QUESTIONS

A. We are most afraid when the circumstances of life are uncertain.

B. When life is interrupted, we want to know for what cause, reason, or purpose.

C. We need to understand the Power of Why.

   1. It can lead to a deeper faith and expand our understanding of God's character and sovereignty.

   2. It can be debilitating when it demands an explanation that we think will restore our control of the circumstances.

II. THE PROMISE OF PEACE

John 16:33

I have told you these things

so that in me you may have PEACE ...

III. PEACE AND THE THINGS JESUS SAID

A. JOHN 13

- An example to follow. (John 13:14-15)

B. JOHN 14

- A better place. (John 14:1-3)

- Clear directions. (John 14:6)

- A self-portrait of God. (John 14:9)

- A direct line to God in prayer. (John 14:13-14)

- Evidence of those who love Him. (John 14:15, 21 & 23)

- The promise of the Holy Spirit. (John 14:25-26)

- His peace is unique. (John 14:27)

C. JOHN 15

- God's design for spiritual growth. (John 15:1-8)

- His joy completes our joy. His joy, like His peace, is unique. (John 15:11)

- A command to love others. (John 15:12-13)

- Hatred from the world. (John 15:18-19)

- More about the Holy Spirit and our mission to point people to Jesus. (John 15:26-27)

D. JOHN 16

- Another warning about mistreatment from the world. (John 16:1-4)

- More about the work of the Holy Spirit and our mission to point people to Jesus. (John 16:7-11)

- Grief will be turned into joy. (John 16:20)

Knowing and practicing the things Jesus said is vital to experiencing the peace He promised.

IV. THE PROMISE OF TROUBLE

John 16:33

**I have told you these things
so that in me you may have peace.
In this world, you will have TROUBLE ...**

A. There is heaven, and there is here. Here is not heaven.

B. The peace Jesus promised can be experienced in the midst of trouble.

V. MORE THAN WE CAN HANDLE

Life is what happens to you while you're busy making other plans.

– From *Beautiful Boy* by John Lennon

A. The Bible doesn't say that God won't give us more than we can handle.

- 1 Corinthians 10:13 // No temptation has overtaken you except what is common to mankind. And God is faithful; he will not let you be **tempted** beyond what you can bear. But when you are tempted, he will also provide a way out so that you can endure it. (NIV)

B. Throughout history, God has given His people more than they can bear.

- The Israelites at the Red Sea.

- Shadrach, Meshach, and Abednego in a fiery furnace.

- David and Goliath.

- Jonah in the belly of a fish.

- The long list of Christians who were persecuted because of their faith.

C. God will give us more than we can handle, but He never gives us more than He can handle.

- God allows us to face impossible obstacles, which gives us the opportunity to deepen our faith, draw close to Him, and discover more about His character and purpose.

VI. FINAL THOUGHTS

A. We can ask God anything, but we need to understand the Power of Why:

- The power to debilitate and derail.

- The power to expand our understanding of God and His purpose.

B. Having all our questions answered will not deliver the peace we need.

- Jesus tells us exactly where to find the peace He promised.

TALK ABOUT IT

1. Think about the power of why to debilitate and derail or expand and deepen. What kind of why questions could we ask in unbearable circumstances to expand our understanding of God's character and sovereignty and deepen our faith?

2. How does the example Jesus set by washing the feet of men who denied, deserted, and betrayed Him help us through relationship trauma?

3. How does it help us in the pain of the present to know that Jesus is preparing an eternal place for us in the future?

4. Jesus promised that He will do whatever we ask in His name. Why do we sometimes think that He's not delivering on His promise?

5. Jesus presented God's design for spiritual growth in John 15. How has God used struggles in the pruning process to make your life more fruitful?

NOTES

NOTES

2

WHERE IS GOD
IN ALL THIS?

LIFE INTERRUPTED

I. THE ELEPHANT IN THE ROOM

   A. We can tell God anything.

- He already knows.

- 1 Peter 5:7 // Cast all your anxiety on him because he cares for you. (NIV)

   B. Two Questions:

- The usual question: WHERE is God in all this?

- The best question: WHO is God in all this?

II. THE SOVEREIGNTY OF GOD

   A. Any sovereign structures that we create will always be imperfect.

   B. God's sovereignty is perfect.

   C. What does it mean for God to be sovereign?

God is in absolute control of His world and everything that happens, without any gaps, limits, interference, or thwarting of His rule.[1] – Paul Tripp

- **Thwart:** frustrating, interrupting, or standing in the way of someone or something by crossing or opposing.

- Our plans may be thwarted or interrupted, but His purpose remains intact without any gaps, limitations, or interference.

D. Two aspects of God's sovereignty:

- His decrees – God's eternal plan. According to His own will and for His own glory, He has decided everything that will come to pass. His decrees are eternal and unchangeable. What God decrees will happen, will happen.

- His providence – God is an active participant. He is in constant contact with the universe that He has made. He governs, sustains, affects, and controls.

He has not set the world in motion and walked away. The motion of the universe is the result of His active sustaining and governing control. He governs the most momentous things in the universe all the way down to the most minor and largely unnoticed things.[2]

– Paul Tripp

- Colossians 1:16-17 // For in him all things were created: things in heaven and on earth, visible and invisible, whether thrones or powers or rulers or authorities; all things have been created through him and for him. He is before all things, and in him all things hold together. (NIV)

---

[1] Paul Tripp, "The Shortest, Most Complex Question," posted September 7, 2022, paultripp.com

[2] Paul Tripp, "The Shortest, Most Complex Question."

E. Jesus understands how hard it is for us to trust and be faithful when everything seems out of control.

- Hebrews 4:15 // For we do not have a high priest who is unable to empathize with our weaknesses, but we have one who has been tempted in every way, just as we are—yet he did not sin. (NIV)

III. LESSONS FROM THE STORY OF LAZARUS

A. Where was Jesus?

- When Jesus received word that his friend Lazarus was sick, He didn't drop what He was doing and rush to his aid.

- John 11:21 & 32 // Lord, if you had been here, my brother would not have died. (NIV)

B. Jesus was received with faith and cynicism.

- John 11:25-27 // "I am the resurrection and the life. The one who believes in me will live, even though they die; and whoever lives by believing in me will never die. Do you believe this?"

  "Yes, Lord," she replied, "I believe that you are the Messiah, the Son of God, who is to come into the world." (NIV)

The life that comes by believing in Jesus is not interrupted by physical death.

- John 11:37 // Could not he who opened the eyes of the blind man have kept this man from dying? (NIV)

C. A bigger picture.

- This was an opportunity for others, like Martha, to believe that Jesus is the resurrection and the life.

- John 11:41-42 // Father, I thank you that you have heard me. I knew that you always hear me, but I said this for the benefit of the people standing here, that they may believe that you sent me. (NIV)

All of the miracles Jesus performed displayed God's power and glory. They were never just about the miracle or the healing.

IV. FINAL THOUGHTS

A. We need a deeper understanding of who God is and who we are.

- Isaiah 55:8-9 // "For my thoughts are not your thoughts, neither are your ways my ways," declares the Lord. "As the heavens are higher than the earth, so are my ways higher than your ways and my thoughts than your thoughts." (NIV)

Functional belief in the doctrine of the sovereignty of God will result in personal humility and a more profound, more genuine spirit of thanksgiving and worship. But it will also produce a confidence in your soul that cannot be shaken.

(continued on next page)

WHERE IS GOD IN ALL THIS? :: SESSION 2

Your Lord never has questions, never is surprised, never is frustrated, never wonders, never is greeted with mystery, never wishes He could have, never looks back with regret, never is hoping, never is waiting, never feels helpless, has nothing He can't figure out, and never finds Himself at a loss.

No one can back God into a corner. He is never pressed to do something. There is no authority over Him that He has to answer to.

In a world that appears so out of control, your confidence will never be found in figuring your life out but in trusting the One who has it all figured out for His glory and your eternal good.[3]

– Paul Tripp

TALK ABOUT IT

1. Have there been times in your life when you wondered, "Where is God in all this?" Describe the circumstances and what you were feeling.

2. In this session, Tierce said we can tell God anything because He already knows, and 1 Peter 5:7 says, "Cast all your anxiety on him because he cares for you." Have you ever been reluctant to tell God what you are thinking? Explain.

3. When Jesus said to Martha, "I am the resurrection and the life," He was revealing who He was in the midst of her pain. How has God revealed who He is in the midst of your pain?

4. Paul Tripp says, *"Functional belief in the doctrine of the sovereignty of God will result in personal humility and a more profound, more genuine spirit of thanksgiving and worship. But it will also produce a confidence in your soul that cannot be shaken."* How has that been true for you?

---

[3] Paul Tripp, "Sovereignty, Humility, and Confidence," posted September 14, 2022, paultripp.com

At the end of this session, Cynthia talked about how naming the things she was grieving and the things she was grateful for helped her process the pain when her life was severely interrupted. These next two pages are here for you.

GRIEF

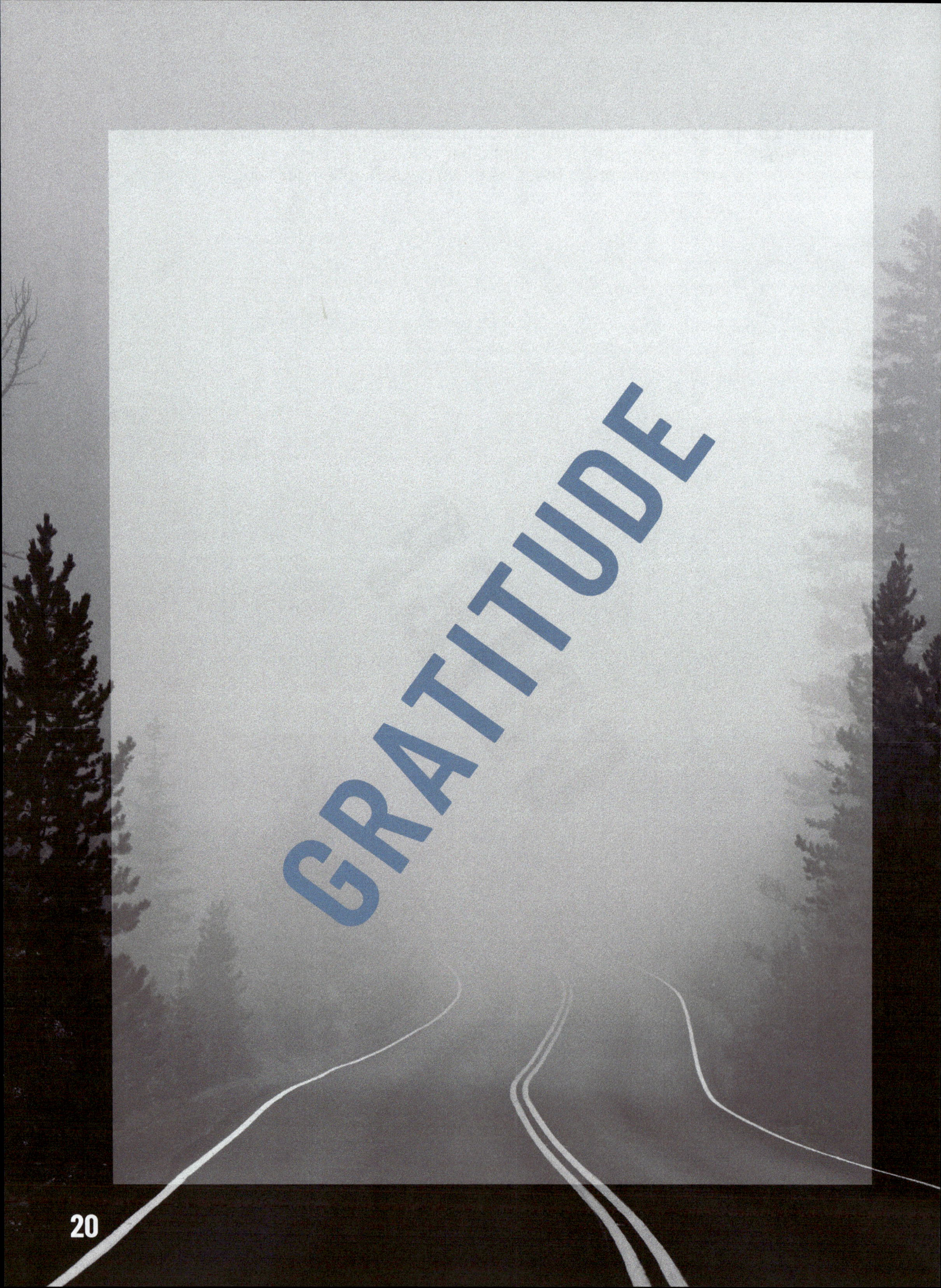

GRATITUDE

3

WHEN LIFE FALLS APART

LIFE
INTERRUPTED

If we could only look upon a difficult crisis as an occasion of bringing out on our behalf the sufficiency of divine grace, it would enable us to preserve the balance of our souls and to glorify God, even in the deepest waters.

— C.H. Mackintosh (1820-1896)

I. A STORY OF UNIMAGINABLE TRAGEDY

A. The Book of Job is not about Good vs. Evil. It raises bigger questions:

- Is it possible that good people could experience horrible pain and selfish people could succeed in God's world?

- If so, what does that say about God's character?

B. In one day, Job lost not some but all of his flocks and herds, all of his servants, and all of his children. (Job 1:13-19)

C. Job's response was inspiring:

- Job 1:20-22 // At this, Job got up and tore his robe and shaved his head. Then he fell to the ground in worship and said: "Naked I came from my mother's womb, and naked I will depart. The Lord gave and the Lord has taken away; may the name of the Lord be praised." In all this, Job did not sin by charging God with wrongdoing. (NIV)

D. Job's body was afflicted with sores from the bottom of his feet to the top of his head. But in all this, Scripture says …

- Job 2:10 // Job did not sin in what he said. (NIV)

II. A LITTLE HELP (AND HURT) FROM HIS FRIENDS

A. Eliphaz, Bildad, and Zophar heard about Job's troubles and came together to comfort him.

- Job 2:12-13 // When they saw him from a distance, they could hardly recognize him. They began to weep aloud, and they tore their robes and sprinkled dust on their heads. Then, they sat on the ground with him for seven days and seven nights. No one said a word to him because they saw how great his suffering was. (NIV)

We don't always need to say something to comfort someone. Don't miss the opportunity to just be in the room and let God's presence be felt in your presence.

B. Job's pain begins to wear him down.

- He curses the day he was born and sounds depressed and hopeless.

- Job 3:24-26 // Sighing has become my daily food. My groans pour out like water. What I feared has come upon me. What I dreaded has happened to me. I have no peace, no quietness. I have no rest but only turmoil. (NIV)

C. The theory of Job's friends was that suffering is a punishment for sin, and prosperity is a reward for righteousness.

- Job 4:7-8 // Who, being innocent, has ever perished? Where were the upright ever destroyed? As I have observed, those who plow evil and those who sow trouble reap it. (NIV)

- Eliphaz strictly connects Job's suffering with something evil he must have done. That's not always the case. The innocent and upright are not exempt from trouble.

[God] causes his sun to rise on the evil and the good, and sends rain on the righteous and the unrighteous. (Matthew 5:45)

Bad things will happen to bad people, but so will good things.
Good things will happen to good people, but so will bad things.

- John 16:33 // I have told you these things so that in me you may have **PEACE**. In this world, you will have **TROUBLE**. (NIV)

D. Eliphaz gives Job a narrow diagnosis and solution.

- Job 5:8; 17 // If I were you, I would appeal to God; I would lay my cause before him … Blessed is the one whom God corrects, so do not despise the discipline of the Almighty. (NIV)

E. Bildad supports the case made by Eliphaz.

- Job 8:5-6 // If you will seek God earnestly and plead with the Almighty, if you are pure and upright, even now he will rouse himself on your behalf and restore you to your prosperous state. (NIV)

F. Eliphaz, Bildad, and Zophar jumped to conclusions and misrepresented God with advice skewed by self-righteousness.

III. JOB'S RESPONSE TO HIS FRIEND'S ACCUSATIONS

A. Excerpts from Job 9:2-28.

- Indeed, I know that this is true. But how can mere mortals prove their innocence before God? Though they wished to dispute with him, they could not answer him one time out of a thousand … Who has resisted him and come out unscathed?

  He moves mountains without their knowing it and overturns them in his anger. He shakes the earth from its place and makes its pillars tremble. He speaks to the sun, and it does not shine. He seals off the light of the stars. He alone stretches out the heavens and treads on the waves of the sea …

  … When he passes me, I cannot see him. When he goes by, I cannot perceive him. If he snatches away, who can stop him? Who can say to him, "What are you doing?" God does not restrain his anger …

  … Even if I summoned him and he responded, I do not believe he would give me a hearing. He would crush me with a storm and multiply my wounds for no reason. He would not let me catch my breath but would overwhelm me with misery. (NIV)

B. Job expressed an incomplete understanding of God through the filter of his own experience.

C. Job implied that God had fallen asleep at the wheel in running the universe, and because of this divine neglect he's had to endure unjust suffering.

D. We see God's incredible patience in allowing us to cry out to Him, even if our way of doing it is misguided.

E. Healing can only begin when we admit what's going on inside.

There can be no healing without revealing.

- Psalm 22:1-2 // My God, my God, why have you forsaken me? Why are you so far from saving me, so far from my cries of anguish? My God, I cry out by day, but you do not answer; by night, but I find no rest. (NIV)

- This is how Jesus felt, and this is how Job felt.

IV. JOB CONSIDERED 3 OPTIONS

A. Put on a happy face!

- Job 9:27-28 // If I say, "I will forget my complaint, I will change my expression, and smile," I still dread all my sufferings … (NIV)

B. What's the point?

- Job 9:29-31 // Since I am already found guilty, why should I struggle in vain? Even if I washed myself with soap and my hands with cleansing powder, you would plunge me into a slime pit so that even my clothes would detest me. (NIV)

C. The need for a mediator.

- Job 9:32-35 // He is not a mere mortal like me that I might answer him, that we might confront each other in court. If only there were someone to mediate between us, someone to bring us together, someone to remove God's rod from me, so that his terror would frighten me no more. Then, I would speak up without fear of him, but as it now stands with me, I cannot. (NIV)

V. JOB'S NEED FOR A MEDIATOR POINTS US TO JESUS

A. Jesus is our mediator.

- 1 Timothy 2:5-6 // For there is one God and one mediator between God and mankind, the man Christ Jesus, who gave himself as a ransom for all people … (NIV)

B. Jesus is a caring and compassionate high priest.

- Hebrews 4:15-16 // We do not have a high priest who is unable to empathize with our weaknesses, but we have one who has been tempted in every way, just as we are—yet he did not sin. Let us then approach God's throne of grace with confidence, so that we may receive mercy and find grace to help us in our time of need. (NIV)

> **The kind of mediator Job wanted was not the kind of mediator he needed.**

TALK ABOUT IT

1. We all need friends who will sit with us in silence while we are experiencing unimaginable pain. Do you have friends like that? Have you been able to be a friend like that for someone who needed comfort? What were the circumstances?

2. The theory of Job's friends was that suffering is a punishment for sin, and prosperity is a reward for righteousness. Is that a common theory today? How have you experienced it? Have you ever thought that you were being punished for something you did?

3. If good people can experience horrible pain and selfish people can succeed in God's world, what does that say about God's character? Does it change who He is?

4. Like Job, we express an incomplete understanding of God through the filter of our own experience. How can that way of thinking be changed?

5. One of Job's options was to put on a happy face (Job 9:27-28). A version of that could be "fake it until you make it." What are the pros and cons of this option?

6. When Job expressed his need for a mediator, he described being afraid of God. If that describes how you feel, ask a trustworthy friend to pray with you about it.

NOTES

NOTES

4

THE MEDIATOR WE NEED

LIFE
INTERRUPTED

Our most passionate prayers are when we are in the most pain.
Superficial prayers are replaced by genuine cries of the heart ...

We draw closer to God by telling him exactly how we feel, not by telling him what we think he wants us to feel.

God wants the real, not the ideal, from you. In pain, you cry out. You argue with God. You complain to God. You express all the negative emotions you're feeling. You don't suppress them. You confess them.[4]

– Rick Warren, *God's Purpose In Your Pain*

I. OUR INABILITY TO MEASURE UP

A. Bildad's description of God's sovereignty and our sinfulness:

- Job 25:2-4 // Dominion and awe belong to God. He establishes order in the heights of heaven. Can his forces be numbered? On whom does his light not rise? How then can a mortal be righteous before God? How can one born of woman be pure? (NIV)

B. King David's understanding of our sinfulness:

- Psalm 51:5 // Surely, I was sinful at birth, sinful from the time my mother conceived me. (NIV)

---

[4] Rick Warren, "God's Purpose In Your Pain," posted March 2, 2023, plough.com

C. The problem with comparing ourselves to others:

- You can always find someone worse than you and feel better about yourself by comparison.

D. Job's problem was not that he didn't think he was *that* bad.

- Job didn't think he was bad *at all*, so why would God allow *him* to suffer?

II. 3 CLAIMS ABOUT GOD AND JOB

A. Jewish scholar Matisyahu Tsevat proposed that the Book of Job explores three claims about God and Job, but only two can be true at the same time:

CLAIM #1	GOD IS JUST AND GOOD
CLAIM #2	THE RETRIBUTION PRINCIPLE
CLAIM #3	JOB'S INNOCENCE

B. Job argued that he had done nothing wrong.

- Job 1:8 // There is no one on earth like him. He is blameless and upright, a man who fears God and shuns evil. (NIV)

C. Like his friends, Job also believed that God rules the world according to the retribution principle, which led him to the brink of an awful conclusion:

- Maybe Claim #1 is false. Maybe God is *not* just or good.

D. What if Claim #1, God is just and good, and Claim #3, Job is innocent, are both true?

- In that case, the Retribution Principle, which states that all suffering is a form of divine punishment and all abundance is a form of reward, is flawed and needs to be exposed.

III. AN INTERLUDE ON TRUE WISDOM

The character of the satan [the adversary] has no power over Job or God. He's like a cardboard cutout whose only role is to raise the questions that are the real focus of this book. Those questions are highlighted for us in the dialogues of Job and his friends, but never resolved. It's only in the central poem of Job 28 that we discover the real message of the book.[5]

– Tim Mackie, The Story of Job – An Ancient Thought Experiment

A. Job 28 takes us on a tour of the earth's riches in search of true wisdom.

B. It declares that it can't be found anywhere on Earth, compared to anything on Earth, and it can't be bought by anything from Earth.

- Job 28:20 // Where then does wisdom come from? Where does understanding dwell? (NIV)

- Job 28:28 // The fear of the Lord—that is wisdom … (NIV)

5 Tim Mackie, "The Story of Job – An Ancient Thought Experiment," posted May 31, 2017, bibleproject.com

IV. THE FEAR OF THE LORD

A. The idea of the fear of the Lord is presented in Proverbs.

- Proverbs 9:10 // The fear of the Lord is the beginning of wisdom, and knowledge of the Holy One is understanding. (NIV)

- The fear of the Lord is not about being afraid of God.

- The fear of the Lord is an attitude of respect and reverence.

B. At this point in Job's life, he was afraid of God.

- Job 9:33-34 // If only there were someone to mediate between us, someone to bring us together, someone to remove God's rod from me so that his terror would frighten me no more. (NIV)

C. Job believed his only hope was for a third party to speak on his behalf.

- Job 9:33 // There is no arbitrator between us, who can place his hand on us both. (NASB)

"Placing his hand on us both" is a gesture of reconciliation, calling for peace. It symbolizes power, implying both parties accept the mediator's authority to settle the case fairly.

V. JOB'S DEMAND AND GOD'S RESPONSE

A. Job demands an explanation:

- Job 31:35 // Oh, that I had someone to hear me! I sign now my defense. Let the Almighty answer me! Let my accuser put his indictment in writing. (NIV)

B. God accuses Job of speaking words without knowledge.

- Job 38:1-3 // Then the Lord spoke to Job out of the storm. He said: "Who is this that obscures my plans with words without knowledge? Brace yourself like a man. I will question you, and you shall answer me." (NIV)

C. God asks Job a series of unanswerable questions and then paints a majestic portrait of His sovereignty.

- Job realizes how unqualified he is and responds …

- Job 40:4-5 // I am unworthy—how can I reply to you? I put my hand over my mouth. I spoke once, but I have no answer—twice, but I will say no more. (NIV)

D. God turns up the heat with irrefutable evidence of Job's inferiority.

- Job finally responds to God with humility.

- Job 42:1-3 // Then Job replied to the Lord: "I know that you can do all things. No purpose of yours can be thwarted. You asked, 'Who is this that obscures my plans without knowledge?' Surely, I spoke of things I did not understand, things too wonderful for me to know." (NIV)

- This began a new life for Job with a deeper understanding of God and His purpose. It was the beginning of true wisdom for Job.

VI. 4 IMPORTANT LESSONS

A. We obey God because He is God, not as a means of earning a blessing or avoiding punishment.

B. God's love, mercy, and justice are not compromised by anything He allows to happen.

- Malachi 3:6 // I, the Lord, do not change. So you, the descendants of Jacob, are not destroyed. (NIV)

- Hebrews 13:8 // Jesus Christ is the same yesterday and today and forever. (NIV)

C. God sees all of eternity as one complete picture, and He is working to accomplish His plan and purpose in every situation.

D. We don't need to know why God does anything because He is God, and we are not.

There may be evil and suffering in the world that, from one perspective, may seem needless, tragic, and unjust. But from a wider vantage point, there may be a vast network of factors that make the same tragedy fit into a larger cause-effect pattern that brings about the saving of many lives. It's impossible for any human to know such things or have such a perspective. This means all of our claims to evaluate God's rule over human history are always limited and will, therefore, fall short.

(continued on the next page)

I don't have a wide enough vantage point to accuse God of incompetence, and I never will. It's an inescapable reality of being human. We are finite, and our brains and sensory abilities are not designed to take in the information necessary to make evaluations of God's choices. We're not God. We're human.[6]

– Tim Mackie, God's Response to Job's Questions About Suffering

VII. FINAL THOUGHTS

A. We are free to ask God questions, but we are never free to question God.

- We are not qualified.

B. The mediator we want is not always the mediator we need.

C. If we only focus on relief from the pain, we might miss God's purpose to reveal Himself to us and the world around us.

D. Remember: There is Heaven, and there is here. And here is not Heaven.

- The view from here is not always clear.

For now, we see only a reflection as in a mirror. Then, we shall see face to face. Now I know in part. Then, I shall know fully, even as I am fully known.   *– 1 Corinthians 13:12*

---

[6] Tim Mackie, "God's Response to Job's Questions About Suffering," posted May 31, 2017, bibleproject.com

TALK ABOUT IT

1. Rick Warren says, "We draw closer to God by telling him exactly how we feel, not by telling him what we think he wants us to feel." How has that been true for you?

2. Our human nature is to compare what we think we deserve to what we think others deserve. What does that reveal about our understanding of our need for a mediator?

3. How do you express a healthy fear of the Lord in your life? How does it affect the way you pray? How does it show up in your life as a husband, wife, son, daughter, friend, boss, or employee?

4. Take a look at the 4 Important Lessons on Page 37. Which ones are difficult to apply?

5. How does knowing that God sees all of eternity as one complete picture and that He is working to accomplish His plan and purpose in every situation provide comfort when things are uncertain?

5

WHY LIFE HURTS

LIFE
INTERRUPTED

■ INTRODUCTION AND REVIEW

A. Remember the Power of Why

- The power to elevate our perspective and expand our understanding of God's sovereignty and purpose.

- The power to limit our thinking, weigh us down, and cause us to drift off course when navigating a storm.

- The wrong side of why requires answers with explanations that restore our control.

B. The Sovereignty of God

- The right side of why is not "WHERE was God in all this?" but "WHO is God in all this?"

- Unanswered doesn't mean unresolved.

Functional belief in the doctrine of the sovereignty of God will result in personal humility and a more profound, more genuine spirit of thanksgiving and worship. But it will also produce a confidence in your soul that cannot be shaken.[7]   – Paul Tripp

[7] Paul Tripp, "Sovereignty, Humility, and Confidence," posted September 14, 2022, paultripp.com

C. The Fear of the Lord

- Proverbs 9:10 // The fear of the Lord is the beginning of wisdom, and knowledge of the Holy One is understanding. (NIV)

- An attitude of humility, respect, and reverence for God.

What comes into our minds when we think about God is the most important thing about us ... The decline of the knowledge of the holy has brought on our troubles. A rediscovery of the majesty of God will go a long way toward curing them. It is impossible to keep our moral practices sound and our inward attitudes right while our idea of God is erroneous or inadequate. If we would bring back spiritual power to our lives, we must begin to think of God more nearly as He is.

– A.W. Tozer, The Knowledge of the Holy

D. An Important Disclaimer:

The peace Jesus promised will not be found in the answers to our questions.

E. The Promise of Trouble

- John 16:33 // ... Here in this world, you will have trouble. But take heart! I have overcome the world. (NIV)

3 REASONS LIFE HURTS

I. OUR OWN CHOICES

A. This is not the same as the Retribution Principle, which holds that good people are blessed and bad people are punished.

B. The Laws of the Harvest

Galatians 6:7-9 // Do not be deceived: God cannot be mocked. A man reaps what he sows. Whoever sows to please their flesh, from the flesh will reap destruction. Whoever sows to please the Spirit, from the Spirit will reap eternal life. Let us not become weary in doing good, for at the proper time we will reap a harvest if we do not give up. (NIV)

- We reap what we sow.

- We reap more than we sow.

- We reap in a different season than we sow.

II. THE CHOICES OF OTHERS

A. Innocent people can find themselves in the blast zone of the bad choices of others.

B. What to expect in the days prior to the return of Jesus:

- 1 Timothy 3:1-5 // There will be terrible times in the last days. People will be lovers of themselves, lovers of money, boastful, proud, abusive, disobedient to their parents, ungrateful, unholy, without love, unforgiving, slanderous, without self-control, brutal, not lovers of the good, treacherous, rash, conceited, lovers of pleasure rather than lovers of God—having a form of godliness but denying its power. (NIV)

- If we find ourselves in a dangerous environment, the best decision may be to get out to protect ourselves and others, especially in a physically abusive relationship.

- Before we look for an exit, we should always look for ways to make adjustments where we are and be an extension of God's grace and truth, to protect the weak and oppressed, and make a positive difference.

> *If I sit next to a madman as he drives a car into a group of innocent bystanders, I can't, as a Christian, simply wait for the catastrophe, then comfort the wounded and bury the dead. I must try to wrestle the steering wheel out of the hands of the driver.* – Dietrich Bonhoeffer

THE MISSION STATEMENT OF JESUS | LUKE 4:18-19

The Spirit of the Lord is on me because he has anointed me to proclaim good news to the poor. He has sent me to proclaim freedom for the prisoners and recovery of sight for the blind, to set the oppressed free, to proclaim the year of the Lord's favor.

C. Staying in a negative environment to protect and influence others will strengthen your faith and bring a blessing.

- John 13:17 // Now that you know these things, you will be blessed if you do them.

- The blessing may not come when we want it or in our preferred package.

- There is no guarantee that others and the world around you will change, but YOU will.

III. THE DAMAGE OF A BROKEN WORLD

A. Pain, disappointment, and frustration.

- Genesis 3:16 // To the woman, he said, "I will make your pains in childbearing very severe. With painful labor you will give birth to children. Your desire will be for your husband, and he will rule over you." (NIV)

- Genesis 3:17-19 // To Adam he said … "Cursed is the ground because of you. Through painful toil you will eat food from it all the days of your life. It will produce thorns and thistles for you, and you will eat the plants of the field. By the sweat of your brow, you will eat your food until you return to the ground, since from it you were taken, for dust you are and to dust you will return." (NIV)

The damage of a broken world is a reminder of our sin and our need for a Savior.

- Romans 8:22 // We know that the whole creation has been groaning as in the pains of childbirth right up to the present time. (NIV)

B.   In the beginning, there was a perfect world, and one day, we'll step into a perfect Heaven without any pain or struggles.

   •   Revelation 21:4 // He will wipe away every tear from their eyes, and death shall be no more, neither shall there be mourning, nor crying, nor pain anymore, for the former things have passed away. (NIV)

C.   We live between what was and what will be, where we will have trouble.

   •   God is always working for our good in the midst of it all.

TALK ABOUT IT

1.   In the story at the end of this session, Lindsay mentioned a couple who went through a similar situation and how God healed their baby. She said, "If them, why not us?" Have you experienced something like this? Explain.

2.   Have you experienced struggles because of your own bad choices? Explain. What steps did you take to stop the pain and get on a healthier path?

3.   Have you been hurt by the choices of others? How did you respond? What, if any, changes in your environment had to be made?

4.   How have you, or someone close to you, been affected by the damage of a broken world?

5.   A.W. Tozer said, *"The decline of the knowledge of the holy has brought on our troubles. A rediscovery of the majesty of God will go a long way toward curing them."* Has that been your experience? How?

NOTES

6

WHAT GOOD IS IT?

PART 1

LIFE
INTERRUPTED

■ INTRODUCTION

A. "Everything happens for a reason" should be an expression of faith in God's sovereignty and His divine plan and purpose.

B. And we know that in all things, God works for the good of those who love him, who have been called according to his purpose. (Romans 8:28)

- **AND WE KNOW**   There's certainty in that. We don't have to guess or wonder or speculate. We don't have to wait for circumstances to resolve. We know, and we know now. There's no doubt. And we know …

- **THAT IN ALL THINGS**   This includes all of our hurts, mistakes, sins, genetics, experiences, and even what others do to us. And we know that in all things …

- **GOD WORKS FOR THE GOOD**   Everything is not good, but God is always working for our good in everything. Anyone can bring good out of good, but God can bring good out of evil.

- **OF THOSE WHO LOVE HIM**   This is not a blanket promise to everyone experiencing pain. It's available to everyone, but not everyone can claim it. If I'm living in rebellion against God's plan for me, or if I reject His love, everything will work toward my destruction and death. The promise of the potential for good from anything is specifically available to those who love Him.

- **WHO HAVE BEEN CALLED ACCORDING TO HIS PURPOSE** The key to finding peace in life's interruptions is understanding God's purpose for our lives and that pain could be a part of it. Only then will we find the good that is promised.

GOOD THINGS TO CONSIDER WHEN LIFE HURTS

I. DIRECTION

A. Our sovereign God has chosen to work with us.

- We plan. He directs.

- Proverbs 16:9 // The mind of a person plans his way, but the Lord directs his steps. (NASB)

Sometimes, your decision is made for you. For example, when a job or college application is rejected, God has likely closed that door. On the other hand, not all obstacles are closed doors. Some are just things you need to overcome as you follow God. Just because a door is open does not mean God always wants you to walk through it.[8]

— Faith Eng & Evangeline Vergo, *How To Know God's Will*

8 Faith Eng & Evangeline Vergo, "How To Know God's Will," cru.org

Many Christians follow the illogical and unbiblical closed-door policy, often with unsatisfactory and frustrating consequences. God's work in our lives does not exclude such experiences, but the closed-door policy refers to a careless hit-or-miss attitude that does not include evaluation of all the issues.[9]

– Bill Bright, Five Steps to Knowing God's Will

B. Clear direction requires constant contact and daily devotion.

- Luke 9:23 // Whoever wants to be my disciple must deny themselves, take up their cross **daily**, and follow me. (NIV)

C. It's easier to steer a moving vehicle and easier to guide a living sacrifice.

- Romans 12:1-2 // I urge you, brothers and sisters, in view of God's mercy, to offer your bodies as a living sacrifice, holy and pleasing to God—this is your true and proper worship. Do not conform to the pattern of this world, but be transformed by the renewing of your mind. Then you will be able to test and approve what God's will is—his good, pleasing, and perfect will. (NIV)

- A course correction is occasionally required to stay in the pocket of God's good, pleasing, and perfect will.

[9] Bill Bright, "Five Steps to Knowing God's Will," cru.org

II. DISCIPLINE

A. We should make the choice to discipline ourselves.

- 1 Corinthians 9:27 // I discipline my body and keep it under control, lest after preaching to others, I myself should be disqualified. (ESV)

- The work of being a disciple and making disciples takes discipline.

B. We should expect God to discipline us.

- Hebrews 12:7-9 // Endure hardship as discipline. God is treating you as his children. For what children are not disciplined by their father? If you are not disciplined … then you are not legitimate, not true sons and daughters at all. Moreover, we have all had human fathers who disciplined us, and we respected them for it. How much more should we submit to the Father of spirits and live! They disciplined us for a little while as they thought best, but God disciplines us for our good in order that we may share in his holiness. (NIV)

- The work of the Holy Spirit convicting and correcting us when we sin is an indicator of relational legitimacy—proof that we are children of God.

God's purpose is not to make us happy.
His purpose is to make us holy.

- Romans 8:29 // For those God foreknew he also predestined to be conformed to the image of his Son … (NIV)

C. Stating the obvious: Discipline is painful.

- Hebrews 12:11 // No discipline seems pleasant at the time but painful. (NIV)

D. Sometimes, extreme measures are required.

- 1 Timothy 1:18-20 // … Fight the battle well, holding on to faith and a good conscience, which some have rejected and so have suffered shipwreck with regard to the faith. Among them are Hymenaeus and Alexander, whom I have handed over to Satan to be taught not to blaspheme. (NIV)

- The objective of this kind of discipline was for them to learn not to blaspheme, truly repent, and tune in to God's heart.

E. God's purpose for discipline.

- Hebrews 12:11 // … No discipline seems pleasant at the time, but painful. Later on, however, it produces a harvest of righteousness and peace for those who have been trained by it. (NIV)

- God's discipline will produce a harvest of righteousness and peace.

- We may not see it in the moment, but later on, it will produce a harvest.

- God's discipline is not always to correct bad behavior.

Continued in Session 7 …

TALK ABOUT IT

1. When have you prayed and made plans, only for your life to be interrupted and your plans had to be changed? Explain.

2. Have there been open doors that God clearly directed you to <u>not</u> walk through?

3. Have there been closed doors where God directed you to keep trying? If so, what happened, and what did you learn?

4. How has God used struggles as discipline to correct your disobedience and rebellion?

5. Share your thoughts on this statement: God's purpose is not to make us happy but to make us holy.

NOTES

7

WHAT GOOD IS IT?

PART 2

LIFE
INTERRUPTED

You WILL have bad times, but they will always wake you up

to the stuff you weren't paying attention to.

– Comedian and Actor, Robin Williams

GOOD THINGS TO CONSIDER WHEN LIFE HURTS

Continued from Session 6 ...

I. DIRECTION

A. Not every open door should be walked through. And a closed door doesn't necessarily mean we're going in the wrong direction. Instead of no, it could mean not now.

B. The Holy Spirit redirected Paul:

- Acts 16:6-7 // Paul and his companions traveled throughout the region of Phrygia and Galatia, having been kept by the Holy Spirit from preaching the word in the province of Asia. When they came to the border of Mysia, they tried to enter Bithynia, but the Spirit of Jesus would not allow them to. (NIV)

- Acts 16:9-10 // During the night, Paul had a vision of a man of Macedonia standing and begging him, "Come over to Macedonia and help us." After Paul had seen the vision, we got ready at once to leave for Macedonia, concluding that God had called us to preach the gospel to them. (NIV)

Life's detours, dead ends, and disappointments are always opportunities to slow down and tune in to the Holy Spirit.

II. DISCIPLINE

A. God disciplines us because He loves us.

- Hebrews 12:10 // God disciplines us for our good, in order that we may share in his holiness. (NIV)

REMEMBER: God's purpose is not to make us happy but to make us holy.

B. Discipline is not always used to correct disobedience and rebellion.

- Discipline also builds endurance and develops our spiritual muscles.

III. DEEPEN OUR FAITH

A. Just like tension and resistance are required to build physical muscles, struggles play the same role in spiritual fitness.

- Romans 5:3-5 // … We rejoice in our sufferings, knowing that suffering produces endurance, and endurance produces character, and character produces hope, and hope does not put us to shame, because God's love has been poured into our hearts through the Holy Spirit who has been given to us. (ESV)

B. The paradox of rejoicing in trials and trouble.

- James 1:2-4 // Consider it pure joy, my brothers and sisters, whenever you face trials of many kinds because you know that the testing of your faith produces perseverance. Let perseverance finish its work so that you may be mature and complete, not lacking anything. (NIV)

- We rejoice because, in time, we will see good results.

> **PARADOX: a seemingly absurd or self-contradictory statement or proposition that, when investigated or explained, may prove to be well-founded or true.**

C. Faith refined by fire.

- 1 Peter 1:6-7 // In all this, you greatly rejoice, though now, for a little while, you may have had to suffer grief in all kinds of trials. These have come so that the proven genuineness of your faith—of greater worth than gold, which perishes even though refined by fire—may result in praise, glory, and honor when Jesus Christ is revealed. (NIV)

- Trials can reveal the flaws and impurities in our faith.

> **When our life is interrupted and shaken, what comes out of us is what's in us.**

D. An urgency to deepen our faith in these last days.

- Matthew 24:6-14 // You will hear of wars and rumors of wars … Nation will rise against nation and kingdom against kingdom … Many will turn away from the faith and will betray and hate each other, and many false prophets will appear and deceive many people. Because of the increase of wickedness, the love of most will grow cold, but the one who stands firm to the end will be saved. And this gospel of the kingdom will be preached in the whole world as a testimony to all nations, and then the end will come. (NIV)

IV. DISPLAY GOD'S POWER AND GRACE

A. Trials and struggles can set the stage for God to display His power and grace.

- John 9:1-2 // As he went along, he saw a man blind from birth. His disciples asked him, "Rabbi, who sinned, this man or his parents, that he was born blind?" (NIV)

- The wrong side of the Power of Why: Why did this happen? Who can we blame?

- The disciples' question was a throwback to the Retribution Principle from the story of Job in Session 4, which holds that good people are always blessed and bad people are always punished.

- John 9:3 // "Neither this man nor his parents sinned," said Jesus, "but this happened so that the works of God might be displayed in him. (NIV)

B. This was an obvious display of God's power and grace.

- John 9:6-7 // After saying this, he spit on the ground, made some mud with the saliva, and put it on the man's eyes. "Go," he told him, "wash in the Pool of Siloam." So the man went and washed, and came home seeing. (NIV)

V. FINAL THOUGHTS

A. There's never a question of God's ability to do something.

B. When life is interrupted, it's always a matter of God's sovereignty and an opportunity to flex our faith and affirm that He is working in all things for the good of those who love Him.

- Ephesians 3:20-21 // Now to him who is able to do immeasurably more than all we ask or imagine, according to his power that is at work within us, to him be glory in the church and in Christ Jesus throughout all generations, for ever and ever! (NIV)

TALK ABOUT IT

1. How has God used trials to reveal flaws and impurities in your faith?

2. How has God used discipline to build spiritual endurance and deepen your faith?

3. How has God displayed His power and grace through struggles in your life and/or others in your life?

4. The stories at the end of this session and Session 5 are connected. The couples are friends, and they all love God. One baby was healed. One baby died. How does God display His power and grace in different outcomes like these?

5. Pray that God will help you trust in His sovereignty and His divine plan and purpose.

NOTES

NOTES

8

FINDING PEACE

John 16:33

I have told you these things so that in me you may have peace.

In this world, you will have trouble.

But take heart! I have overcome the world.

■ INTRODUCTION

A. Two promises:

- The promise of peace.

- The promise of trouble.

B. There is no transactional formula for finding peace.

C. The peace Jesus promised is in a class of its own.

- John 14:27 // Peace I leave with you. My peace I give you. I do not give to you as the world gives. Do not let your hearts be troubled, and do not be afraid. (NIV)

- His peace is not affected by our circumstances or pain level.

D. The Apostle Paul's unexpected discovery:

- 2 Corinthians 12:9-10 // But he said to me, "My grace is sufficient for you, for my power is made perfect in weakness." Therefore, I will boast all the more gladly about my weaknesses so that Christ's power may rest on me. That is why, for Christ's sake, I delight in weaknesses, in insults, in hardships, in persecutions, in difficulties. For when I am weak, then I am strong. (NIV)

We must be ready to allow ourselves to be interrupted by God ... We must not assume that our schedule is our own to manage, but allow it to be arranged by God.

– Dietrich Bonhoeffer

FINDING PEACE

I. THE PEACE OF GOD IS IN THE WORD OF GOD

A. Jesus connected the peace He promised with things He said.

- "I have told you these things ..."

- The peace Jesus promised is connected to all of God's Word.

- 2 Timothy 3:16-17 // All Scripture is God-breathed and is useful for teaching, rebuking, correcting, and training in righteousness so that the servant of God may be thoroughly equipped for every good work. (NIV)

B. God's Word reveals His character and nature, His sovereignty and power, that He is holy and just, faithful and unchanging.

It's vital for us to understand not WHERE God is in difficult situations but WHO He is in every situation.

C. God's character is personalized in the self-portrait of Jesus.

- John 14:8-9 // "Lord, show us the Father, and that will be enough for us."

  Jesus answered: "Don't you know me, Philip, even after I have been among you such a long time? Anyone who has seen me has seen the Father. (NIV)

D. God's Word helps us stay in sync with His plan and purpose and in the right position to experience His peace.

- Joshua 1:8 // Keep this Book of the Law always on your lips. Meditate on it day and night so that you may be careful to do everything written in it. Then, you will be prosperous and successful. (NIV)

E. Meditating on God's Word changes the way we act by changing the way we think.

- Memorize it.

- Personalize it.

- Pray it.

If your law had not been my delight, I would have perished in my affliction. I will never forget your precepts, for by them, you have preserved my life.

Psalm 119:92-93

II. THE PEACE OF GOD IS IN TIME ALONE WITH GOD

A. Don't get lost in the mechanics of daily devotions and miss God's plan, purpose, and peace.

- Matthew 23:27-28 // Woe to you, teachers of the law and Pharisees, you hypocrites! You are like whitewashed tombs, which look beautiful on the outside but on the inside are full of the bones of the dead and everything unclean. In the same way, on the outside, you appear to people as righteous, but on the inside, you are full of hypocrisy and wickedness. (NIV)

B. We need the noise-canceling practice of a genuine daily time alone with God.

- Philippians 4:6-7 // Do not be anxious about anything, but in everything, by prayer and petition, with thanksgiving, present your requests to God. And the peace of God, which transcends all understanding, will guard your hearts and your minds in Christ Jesus. (NIV)

C. Time alone with God takes TIME.

- If you don't *have* the time, *make* the time.

III. THE PEACE OF GOD IS IN COMMUNITY WITH THE PEOPLE OF GOD

A. We need "God with skin on."

- 1 Corinthians 12:26 // If one part suffers, every part suffers with it. If one part is honored, every part rejoices with it. (NIV)

- Romans 12:15 // Rejoice with those who rejoice, weep with those who weep. (NIV)

B. Don't miss the opportunity to just be in the room and let God's presence be felt in your presence.

> *Pain is the great equalizer because it is indiscriminate. Pain pays no attention to status, wealth, religion, education, age, or gender. Loss is a universal common denominator. So, if you want to draw others closer to you in fellowship, dare to be vulnerable. That requires being honest with God and yourself first. It requires allowing others to see you in your pain and to bear your burden.*[10]
>
> *– Rick Warren, God's Purpose for Your Pain*

C. God has designed us to laugh with each other in the good times, walk with each other in the difficult times, and hold each other in the terrible times.

- Proverbs 17:17 // A friend loves at all times, and a brother is born for a time of adversity. (NIV)

---

[10] Rick Warren, "God's Purpose In Your Pain," posted March 2, 2023, plough.com

IV. THE PEACE OF GOD IS IN THE SON OF GOD

A. The peace we need is not found in answers to our questions that restore our control.

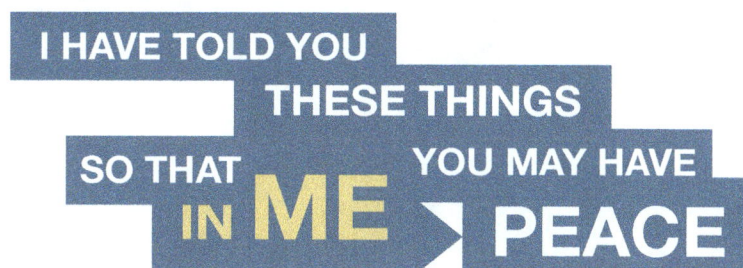

I HAVE TOLD YOU THESE THINGS SO THAT IN **ME** YOU MAY HAVE **PEACE**

B. Instead of running to the answers to our questions, we need to run to Him.

C. God will allow life to be interrupted by detours that take us to a place where we'll reach the end of ourselves and have the opportunity to draw near to Him.

- James 4:8 // Draw near to God, and he will draw near to you. (NIV)

- In moments like this, we realize that what we can't do, God is already doing.

Complaining to God when you're in pain is a biblical act of worship—it's called lamenting. One-third of the 150 psalms in the Book of Psalms are psalms of lament. Worship is not always celebration, praise, and thanksgiving. Expressing every aspect of grief—shock, sorrow, struggle, surrender—can bring you closer to God. All your emotions are God-given. You have emotions because you're made in God's image, and God is an emotional God.[11]

– Rick Warren, God's Purpose for Your Pain

---

[11] Rick Warren, "God's Purpose In Your Pain," posted March 2, 2023, plough.com

> May God, in His mercy, lead us through these times,
> but above all, may He lead us to Himself.
>
> – Dietrich Bonhoeffer

TALK ABOUT IT

1. How have you found the peace of God in the Word of God? What are some of your go-to scriptures?

2. What challenges have you faced with finding peace in God's Word? (Struggles with developing the habit of reading it? Struggles with understanding it? What else?)

3. Do you have the noise-canceling practice of time alone with God? What does it look like for you? How do you find solitude with just you and God?

4. Do you have a community of trustworthy relationships with whom you can bare your soul? How did those relationships begin? How has God used struggles to build deeper relationships?

5. James 4:8 says, "Draw near to God, and He will draw near to you." Have you experienced that? How?

6. If you're hurting, ask God to help you express every aspect of your grief and not hold anything back. Make space for Him to step into your circumstances and do what only He can do. Ask God to help you identify someone you can trust to share your burden.

NOTES

PERSONAL APPLICATION

Information without application leads to frustration. Use this page to write down a few practical and personal steps to help you apply the principles from this series.

The goal is transformation, not behavior modification. The practice of writing down a plan with goals and steps will put you in a better position to experience God's purpose and the life Jesus promised.

Share your plan with a trustworthy friend who will support and pray for you.